Fast Girls Wear Loud Colors

poems

NICHOLE O. NICHOLS

Olette Media, LLC
nichole@nicholeonichols.com
www.nicholeonichols.com

ISBN: 978-0692875940
Library of Congress Control Number: 2017911568

First Printing,2017

Editor: Amanda Chambers
Cover Designer: Joshua Henry Jenkins

CONTENTS

PRE-MATTER/
THE ELEMENTS

Before color, there are the elements. They build us. Physically, they comprise the skin over our flesh, the bones that prop us up, the eyes that see our world at face value, and the ears that hear what wasn't supposed to be heard. Spiritually, they are the foundation of our emotions and our personalities. They are the frequencies on which our thoughts travel. We all swirled in pieces through the star-dusted darkness of heaven as we waited for God to pull our parts together and line our mothers' wombs with us. We are born, and then life colors us, loudly.

Fast Girls Wear Loud Colors

CARBON

Birth
It is when you exhale
And put your first carbon
Out into the air
As a loud, shouting thing
Carbon is essential to life
You either eat to digest to make carbon
Or you are digested to make carbon
You matriculate through school
One graphite filled, state mandated bubble at a time
You gasp as a man puts a shiny piece
of carbon on your finger
You laugh as your kids unwrap gifts on a frosted night
In a house warmed by the by-products
Of a pre-dawn era
Or
You are alone
In an apartment
Surrounded by your own carbon
Carbon is soft and hard
Black and clear
Worthless and precious
At the same time
Birth
Is when the stark contrasts
Of life
Scare you and comfort you
At the same time

Fast Girls Wear Loud Colors

TUNGSTEN

There are two foolish approaches to death
One is arrogant denial
The other is allowing the inevitability
To punk you
Into forfeiting your living years
To safety

Tungsten
Produces more heat than light
You talk too much
You fret too much
You hope too much
You sit on torn upholstery in a dusty corner
Tungsten
Anchoring you in place
And in complacence
You don't understand your power
You don't understand...
The tungsten plating your bones and veins
Is what you use to push
Lean into the hardness
You are alloy
You are alright

COBALT

The flashing slab of glass and metal
That has seduced you into a waking sleep
Is powered by a blue stone
Deep Zambia blue
Royal Congo blue
It is convenient and now the standard
To package delicate and thorny conversations
In blue or green bubbles
And send them through a slate grey iClouded digital sky
To their intended parties
With the tap of a finger pad on glass
Cobalt makes that happen
Cobalt has a hand in intercepting that same finger pad
From touching the face of the receiver
Once those blue or green bubbles
Have burst forth their shrapnel
Decorated with smiling, tearful emojis
Into the receiver
Cobalt says "take it easy"
Tap and go
Cobalt makes a mess
In large quantities it is carcinogenic
In large quantities, text based relationships
Rip the sinew between us
Erode the membrane within our foundations
Make us battery operated
Blue stone dominated
And in its radioactive form
Cobalt can heal us
Tracing the cancer back to its origin
Us
You've used 90% of your data for this month.

Fast Girls Wear Loud Colors

HYDROGEN

You asked me for ice water
In a fluted glass
I poured it up for you
And watched
As the droplets ran from the corners of your lips
Down the sides of your chin
And dampened the collar of your shirt
You asked me for the sun, sky diamonds
You asked me for Saturn's icy, stone-studded rings
Hydrogen
You asked me to unbond the hydrogen
In my veins
And hand it off to you
So that you could make water of me
Since you are still thirsty
All that hydrogen + oxygen + hope + waiting
Will not quench you
I cannot baptize you
I will not untangle my molecules
And my lacy equilibriums for you
You are Jupiter's storm

OXYGEN

You only think of me when you need me
In
Out
In
Out
Lungs exchange in respiration
Taking oxygen from the fresh lushness
Of the rainforest that I am dressed in
I am photosynthetic
I snatch the by-products of your breath
From clear air + light
And patch together my own meals
Oxygen
Makes up half of the Earth's crust
Two-thirds of your body
And you balance on a teetering scale
Of life and self combustion everyday
You only think of me when you need me
Until you're snuffed out by my absence
Or seared from my overflow.

LITHIUM

She packed a distressed leather bag
With two pairs of pants
Two t-shirts
Four pairs of panties
And one bra
She unzipped a small hot pink cosmetic bag
And tucked two tubes of lipstick
One red and one pink
A small bottle of medium coverage foundation in Chestnut
Some Ardell lashes
And a harsh black eyeliner
Inside the bag in the folds
Of its gold satin lining
She inspected herself
In the mirror on the back of the
Bathroom door
She searched
Under smooth brownness
Past eyes glittering with wit
Through immaculate bone structure
Through roundness and leanness
Perfectly placed
She searched and found
Flaws that weren't there yesterday
They weren't there this morning
They weren't there two hours ago
Lithium
They like to tell her that she's crazy
When she starts to make sense
Lithium is toxic in large doses

Lithium has no known biological role
They give her lithium to rid her
Of her inconvenient emotions
Created by her inconvenient revelations
She is not ok
And that is alright
For once, she is allowed to let her seams split

NEON

I've been trying to figure out the glow for a while now
I've been trying to capture it
Extract its ingredients
So that I can fold them into my own layers
and feel the warmth that only comes
From knowing you've risen to the challenge
Of your purpose
I thought I could study it
Save for it in a porcelain star shaped bank
Talk my way into it
Trade my sleep hours for it
Wade into it
But the glow is neon
Neon will not react with any other substance
Colorless
Odorless
Tasteless
Unmovable
Noble
And the only signs with pure neon
Glow red
You'll know it when you see it

RADON

You seeped in from the ground
And slowly convinced me
Mutated me
Into another being
I thought I knew myself
Until I met you
I thought I could trust myself
Until I ran into you
You healed me
By implanting yourself deep within a tumor
That you placed behind a veil of
Nerves, membranes, flesh
You broke down the tumor
That you created
And you threaten
To grow within me
A new mass
Malignant this time

SULFUR

I smell the sulfur from the highway
As we pass a paper mill tucked within
Evergreen trees, poplars, elms
Pulp
Whitened by sulfur because we are used to white paper
Refined
And that refinement stinks
We enter the world as thorny, grainy, splintered things
We are sanded
Watered down
Flattened
Whitened
But then we reminisce about when we were trees
When the only sulfur we knew was drawn up from the soil
By our roots
To nourish us
To build our proteins
That same sulfur rains down on us in another form
Leaching us
Starving us

PEACH/INNOCENCE

The little girl never leaves us. She becomes more refined. She learns how not to get burned. She learns how to wear heels. She learns that her hair, her makeup, her clothes, and her body fat percentage are her worth, in some people's eyes. She learns that cooking, cleaning, and coitus are her worth in other people's eyes. She learns to walk the perimeter. She learns how to erase her own voice. She learns what the rules are. She learns how to break them. She learns a lot, but she never leaves. She still sits in the hammock of your gut waiting for your permission.

SWEET GIRL

Birthdays used to be sacred
On my 5th, I twirled around the den
Of a split-level house
In a peach dress
As an effervescent type of static
Ran through my veins
In anticipation of my first
Party
Everyone was there
And I wanted them there
We ate Detroit-style pizza together
We slid across waxed wooden floors
On decade old skates together
We were sweet girls
Like the packets of sugar
That when ripped apart
Would dump a sweetness
Into the cold brown brew our mothers were drinking
Real sugar clumps in the bottom of the glass
We wore our hair in triple plaits
One in front and two in the back
We insisted on wearing purple tights
With a red skirt and an orange sweater
On the first day of school
Our unpruned thoughts
Bubbled up from the pits of us
And floated from our mouths
"Ain't she cute!"
We learned to redact ourselves
We learned to truncate ourselves
We learned to put on that black skirt suit,
Undo our three plaits

Fast Girls Wear Loud Colors

Dollop them with a lye-based cream
Wash it out and ignore the red, scaly patches
We learned to wear our pearls around our necks
Not to decorate ourselves
But so that they can always be counted and accounted for
At will
At random
We serve them pleasantries
"Smile!"
"Why don't you smile?"
"I need to see you smiling!"
They ask us to smile even when they are blocking the sun
We were born as sugar
We were not willing to dissolve
We are now Sweet N Low
We dissolve quickly
We dissolve quickly

PINK & GOLD

I used to want a three-foot plastic house with an elevator
That was operated by a pull cord with a purple handle
Pink siding,
Pink hollow furniture,
And stickers for wallpaper

My girlhood was painted
Pink and gold
I thought that my
Small veined hand
That offered half of my lunchtime
Portion of Oreos
Would always be
Reciprocated

I thought that the boy who played
House with me
Would one day stretch his arms
Around me
And send the note back
With the box checked "yes"

I thought that I would always
Be able to take the noise in the back room for granted
That it would always
Rise up from bodies
That doted on me

I thought that finding out
How many apples
Mark had if he had 7 and ate 2
Would pay off one day

Fast Girls Wear Loud Colors

I thought that high school hallways
Were long and wide
But they are
Short, narrow
Following their tiles
Leads some to gravel
Some to compost
Some to marble
And we all come back
10 years later
Devastated by how quickly we went
And how far away we are
Our eyes squint at years
That pour forth like
Tides under new moons
And the salty froth
That the white squall leaves behind
Is called nostalgia
The sun that rises
Gold in its heat
Washes the sky in somewhat of a mauve
And reveals that my pink dream house
Always had flimsy plastic pink siding,
Pink hollow furniture,
and stickers for wallpaper

RABBIT EYES

1. Grandma told me that the new soreness on my chest
Came from my set of rabbit eyes
Red, probing
They pushed through
Some girls wore larger sweatshirts
Avoided playing games that involved jumping
I wore fitted shirts
Played with jump ropes
And hopped over backs while playing jump frog

Boys with cackling voices
And dotted faces

Girls with bodies
Still waiting on
Dormant womanhood

They peeked through

Mama took me shopping
For bras because an undershirt
No longer contained them

Two cloth triangles
Joined at the bottom
With a band
And two straps at the top of each
To hold them both onto my chest
Lace
Color
A then B

Then 34 C
Rapidly

2. I wasn't done being a girl yet at 12
But during a bathroom break in 6th grade
I pulled down my pants and saw
Red
Rabbit eyes on my chest
Red in my pants
Pain in my back
Weight in my thighs
My hands, numb
Stares in the hall
I focused on looking straight ahead
As I walked back to my class in a single file line
No one pointed out
The red stains on the back of my
Second hand silk shorts set.

3. Promiscuity
Is a function of
Colored panties x Puberty ÷ Boys Who Will Be Boys
But Girls Who Will Be Girls
Must always wear white panties
Captivating, isn't it?
The hydrangeas spread their periwinkle clusters
As bees crawl over each velvet-petaled sphere
With yellow dusted legs
Pollinators are seduced by color
And thank God for that
Because many church perimeters and proper Down East gardens
Would never yield their
Greens
Blackberries for preserves

Or dew drenched white peonies
For Sunday's dinner table
Without Color.
Purple, Red, Pink
Means come to me
Means I'm ready to unravel and feel the nectar
Run down my thighs
And feel the follicle
Burst forth
And announce itself
As a pang in my back
As a pinch in my side
Her mother wouldn't allow
Colored panties in her house
But that didn't stop her from dripping
Technicolor
And blooming defiantly
Delightedly.

RED/ADOLESCENCE

Of all of the colors, red is considered by our grannies and aunties to be the fastest color of them all. To them, red means a warning. It is the color of dishonored families, broken social mores, and disrespected traditions. After all, the letter on Hester's chest was scarlet. Red isn't a warning; it's an announcement. Girls sneak and wear red when they want to be noticed. Red is an experiment. It talks back. And what will you do about it?

THIS SUMMER 7-3-00

Summer from Egypt
Lyricist weather
Waves rise in the day
Take a Polaroid
More like a hymn
Summer's the little bridge
A lapse of blank time
Pure clarity
Before the rigidness that
Autumn brings
This year it brings another phase
Of whatever journey this might be
Right now I just want to
Drown in Summer
Inhale it all
And swallow it
And push negativity far away
Maybe to Antarctica

Fast Girls Wear Loud Colors

ROYAL CHERRY

Royal Cherry
Beats in my heart like streams
Rivers
Cascade over
My head
My hips
My feet
And washes me ashore
To cough up my seaweed-tangled
Spirit
My pit
And it is gone as the sun is
Beneath the ink of the night

ORIGINALITY

Can I be an original?
Can I cast my own light?
Will I weave my own picture?
Or is everything connected
Prenatally
Eternally
For High Plans I don't understand?

UNREQUITED

Love seems to be pretty wonderful
I wouldn't know
I never got any
The closest I got was
Crushes that constricted me
Made my blood sparkle
Put me on the edge
Of the bigger thing
 I wish I got to feel it
Love seems to be pretty horrible
I wouldn't know
I never got any
The closest I got was
A broken hope
That died whenever
The crush turned upside down
Made the marrow of my bones hurt
Sent me to the edge
Of the bigger thing
I'm glad I never got to feel it

INSIDE THE LINES

Just as I am sitting here
I know that there are those
Who are beyond my human touch
No technology, with all its
Digital glory and microchip sequins,
Can let me get to the place where
They are...
And just as I was thinking
I changed my mind
Had time to assess what I
Was doing
And canceled the action
Because I know it's outside
Of my lines
To sit here in sorrow
For something that isn't sorrow

Fast Girls Wear Loud Colors

GREEN

Why do I
Drip drop
Green
Like a willow
In the rain
The only thing keeping me
From lysis
Is Natural God
In my brain,
I cry in the hollow forest
My own words come back to me
I stand and wait
For the prince to save me,
But he chose Rapunzel instead
She had Indian hair
And Chinese eyes
And wasn't an everyday
Negro woman like me
Dewdrops frost
And I become frigid
Ice cubed
But ever dreaming of the day
When my never-ending story ends
And I receive
This kiss that takes the
Poison away

GREEN PART 2

Drip drop
Green
Like a willow
In the rain
Slowly slip
Into the quicksand
Realize quick
Landslides come slick
Trips up those
That weren't steady
Flip flop
Goes the bird
Expired

Fast Girls Wear Loud Colors

WOMANHOOD

I'm on the brink of womanhood
It's hazy
Like a summer night
Lazy
But I can see brightly
What is reflected
On me to be

TIA

She was never
As pretty as she
Thought she was
And I ain't saying
That I was the prettiest
But I was courteous
Studious
And I know what my
Duty is...
My baby ain't been
Born yet
My job ain't been styled yet
But I know
I won't be kept
Not the keeping kind
I am something so singular
Like a prism
I am one light
Out of many
But pretty is a box
I rebuke
Beauty is a virtue
Of many flavored languages
And pretty is a
Double threat:
Killer + rapist

Fast Girls Wear Loud Colors

ANSWER ME

Answer me. I'm tired of sending ships a sail in waters tepid with indifference. Love and unrequited are braided together like alopecia causing Deep Kinky Wave. Tight like I want my abs.

Answer me. Why do I call and hear your voice recorded so eloquently for me to be avoided? Why do I write pages like this one instead of melting my mindbodysoul into the many higher heights of the world and sky?

Answer me. Eyes see me, but lips stay saliva glued and tongue stays lazy in its wet bed. Dismissed. Not missed but dismissed. Not kissed but dismissed. Not sensed but dismissed and this shit makes me listless.

You can't speak?

Why are you a Titan to me, but I'm a petri dish fool to you?

Answer ME!

Maybe I'm too small for you to notice when I move.

APPLES ARE BLUE

I don't feel like climbing
Through epics and
Iliads
And I hate the slight prick
Of theorems turning side ways
Edging themselves through the creases
In the gray matter that controls me
They have the nerve to
Fluff a pillow and make themselves at home
Right next to the image
That I have of myself
Responding on stage to the
Latest lyrical threat
Issued by the latest one verse wonder
$A2 + B2 = C2$
I see squares
They are these people
That you think should matter so much
To me
DuBois, Booker T, belle hooks
Ntozake, Ishmael Reed, Richard Wright
And two girls named Toni
Cade Bambara and Morrison
What about Braxton?
'Cause now I know who
You're talking about
She's the one with the show on WE
You know, the one I watch on
My phone
While you're talking about

Things that are not on TV
Things that are not online
Things that are not on the radio
Things that won't go viral
Things that aren't as suicidal
To this gray thing in my skull
That you say I'm wasting
Like fast food French fries
That aren't hot enough
Or perfectly good pants
That aren't tight enough
But why should I care?
Success has already been
Painted gold for me
Iced out for me
Black carded
And weaved tight
For me
And all I have to do is say
Yes
Apples are blue
If that's what my flat screen says
Must be true
And Eve's black mamba
Snickers once again.

Aquamarine/Young Womanhood

Your twenties are your laboratory years. They are supposed to be the best time of your life. We don't expect the awkwardness of our preteen years to show its face, and many times we're shocked to find out that the haziness that surrounded the picture of our adulthood in our minds as elementary school aged kids is still there, hanging in the atmosphere. We spend most, if not all, of our twenties trying to figure out how to adjust our fog lamps so that the light that bounces off of this haze doesn't blind us any further. Clarity is a virtue.

LIGHT EVERYWHERE

Everywhere/Everywhere/Sunlight
Everywhere/Binding/Whitening
Never too much or any to spare
The sun touches me
 Inner, Outer, Over, Under
I need every
Point of light
Not out of
Spite do I hoard it
But it makes me feel like
Someone again/ Me/ Free
Like peace doves and wild ivy
Sun/Light/Reflect
Through me.

Fast Girls Wear Loud Colors

BROWN

Your eyes
Have God's signature
And the brownness
Is a smooth ride
To forever
You carry night
On your skin
The stars of the galaxies
Form your outline
You've become the only
Constellation I see
And if my eyes
Become jaded to
The radiance of
Your court of stars,
Lead me softly
Because my dreams kiss you
And the high tide of my ocean
Is reaching to your night
Don't run
Because remember
That you started this
And don't doubt me
Your whole essence
Is beautiful
And I want its long kiss

COLORS IN THE SILENCE

Between my lips
I can work the stagnant silence
In the air
Into lyric colors
My thoughts dance
Like fire in the wind

KNOW ME

If I let you know me
It would be more
Than just a thrill night
To me
My hull would be broken
And you'd have my token
Unredeemable
My life would change
Within every second you knew me
You would see
So much into me
To my soft pulp
My rose color
My starred eyes
My dream alive
Wind and tears
I'm reluctant
To step into you
And let you have
Such a big part of me
I come apart easily
And whoever knows me
Must have strong arms
To hold me together
Knit me back again
And never sail away

PURPOSE DRIVEN
MOSQUITOES

I sleep
As mosquitoes
Sit on my cheeks
And I itch
Scratch
Until the scab is deep
Deep enough to reach
My dreams
Dreams that once were
Healthy
Full of life
Now wounded
The scab is sore
But like soldiers they bare
Bullet holes and rise
Purple hearts and all
Rise like heat
Over the cold front
To the sun
The sun
Makes me sticky as
I sleep
And mosquitoes sit
On my cheeks
Making me itch
Like dreams desiring to be real

Fast Girls Wear Loud Colors

WHAT I'M USED TO

I'm used to writing words
To inexplicable feelings,
Putting names to intangible objects,
I'm used to giving birth
To living verse
Mixing soul and blood and
Enigma like the moon
Together to make
A liquid wide as an ocean
Humble as a puddle
Moves you like a high tide
Waves
Ripples in me like a drop
Hitting still water
I'm used to feeling like
I understand the clouds
Ride on them down a
Beam of sunlight
But only in my mind
They're untouchable
Irretrievable
Like stars, broken promises
Or wasted minutes
Golden opportunities
Tarnished
Now you...
What are you used to?
Ordinary things going
Ordinary ways
Miracles unborn
Or maybe dreams gone astray?
Believe an inch, it is a mile

BLACKGIRL

My skin is a shade darker
Than beauty
They put me on a lower rung
Of womanhood
Than I wanted to be
But I can't complain
My instinct is to
Define myself
I listen to the voices behind me
To control the world before me
Iron grace
Is what has formed in me

MORNING PAPER

The newspaper
Reads like an oracle
Solemn and true
Paper pale like death
Printed ink
Dark like a dead end
At midnight
Cold objectivity
Like ice freezes the page
As stab after stab
Shot after shot
Stop
Don't leave me here
To die and
My life be condensed
To a headline
On newsstands today
Get my soul
My story of my life
Gone
"And she said she didn't want to be
trapped between the hard, black
print and the pale page," the
witness said.

SNOWMAN

I'm by myself again
Sitting in a clutch
Of misery
Not wanting to look
Reality in her face
But slap her down
She'll still get up
And push me forth
Into the winds that
I dread
Hard
Like royal purple
Bruises knotted up
Like balls of spikey sorrow
Knotted up
He's gone
Like the snowman that
Always melted too soon
He's gone
And I sit behind the hole
In the winter ground
Trickling
By myself
By myself again

Fast Girls Wear Loud Colors

DIMEPIECE

She's a fine girl
Black and mild
Coffee curves
Sweet cream
Baby hair
Diamond eyes
Ripe lips
Peach
Strawberry
Flavored kiss
Brand name beauty
Untouchable
Impossible
For us to be
Like the fumes of
A dream
Wafting, transparent
We are real
And a digital pixel
Has no soul
We are fertile ground
Not a dimepiece
But priceless

A PAINTED LIE

I am homeless
Within a mansion
Breathing almost
Still and even
Strings of wind
Maintaining
A fabricated
Silence
A lie
That's not only white
But painted pretty
Oranges that melt
Into pinks and golds
Pretty
But false like time
Let it slide
Make a homerun
Slither away with the
Dream
For it is we who are lost
I am lost
In the valley
Of the home that's mine

Fast Girls Wear Loud Colors

HOMEWORK

You can understand
Poems written 500
And 1000 years ago.
Mathematical Theorems
Logical Laws
Of Nature and Science
That defy imagination
With mazes of intellectual
Pathways and endpoints
But you don't understand
Me
You can pose a question
Complex like a spectrum
But your vocals become
Arid to the touch of
Words for me
Intellect stole your passion
From within my womb
I am here with you
Now
Blood and breath
Feminine
Why can't you search me
Like the solution of X?
Why can't you caress me
With your mind
As you do those
Dusty theories?
Why can't you solve me?
Your infinite numeral
Prime and indivisible

HOW DO I TELL HIM

I don't mean to be
Closed off
But I'm very
Self-conscious
And it seems like
The world stares at me
With one large
Brown pupil
Other times I am
Dust
Thrown to the wind
Insignificant
The world shatters
Across my inner
Fiber
And yet how can I
Feel this way
When I am in reality
Somewhere in between
The real issue is
How can I tell him
What everyone else seems
To say with ease?
The numbered fire
In the sky
Says only half
Of what I feel
I raise my hand
To the sun and
I am cold
The world flies daily
But mine has stopped

Because I'm tired
Of looking past the moment
To a better horizon
That never comes
I am red with affection
Full of it and bloated
But nowhere to dispose of it
Rather, no one to give it to
I say
I don't say
And what I don't say
Harms me greatly
Through and through
I feel the absence
Of those words vibrate
And reverberate off my psyche
Echoes of lostness
But what is holding me?
Hungry eyes I fear will be
The end of my virtue's soul
No

Fear of being judged
And turned away
To make love to the snow
So
How can I tell him?
If?
When?
Where?
How do I tell him?

DAYTIME MINUTES

Daytime minutes
Do they come in bulk
Days, hours
Or do they pass
More like seconds
Grains fallen
To the bottom
Of the glass
And yet we devour them
Like we expect more
To follow
We descend into
Our nighttime hour
And expect them
To carry over
No
They won't
They'll stay unused
Uncherished
Locked
Forever
Yes, this is phone jargon
Referring to the instrument
That causes so much
Detachment
We protect those minutes
Against wasting them on
Family, friends...

Fast Girls Wear Loud Colors

Not knowing how many
Minutes we have
How many minutes
They have
Or if we'll ever see
Or speak to them
Again
-Click-

HALFLIFE

The Dirty Bombs
They are the things
That take us out
As lightning does
Swiftly
Rudely
Cold heat
Fills the cells that
Once held
All your creation
They are quiet
Beneath our skin
Transmitted by every
Neuron
And immune to every
Lymph Node
They live long
Long after the forest burns
Ashes seeded
Planted
Grown into brush to
Be burnt again
Like radiation
Radon and Uranium
Even the ion
Buried beneath
Echoes its jeopardy ray
50,000
50,000,000 years
Into the universe
They kill
Terrorize

And they pluck life away
Like a serial murderer
On a fantasy spree
Kingpin
Out to collect today
Selfishly
Deadly exchange
They pin to the wall
And rape like pedophiles
They watch the young
Pink ripen
Just to corrode them
They stab and scrap
Let blood into
The street for
Strays to lap up
And spit up in the morning
'cause it's vile
They leave us to die...
They leave us to die
And they are whispered
Everyday into the
Flowering ear of another
Spreading like a carnivorous rash
And the victim is left
To die
From the inside out
Carin beetles come
to play

HOME

When I write
I'm sitting in the
Twilight
Of my own fear
I put it in a web
Of words
And the light shines
A rainbow
Through it
To make beautiful
What was hideous
Freedom is in
These lines
And I'm home
When I write.

LOVE

Whatever calms me down
And rouses me
Whatever feeds me and
Puts me through a
Famine unlike death
Whatever frees me,
Enslaves me,
Whatever snatches
The blood from my veins
And pushes the Nile
Through them
Whatever heals me
Hurts me
Gives to me
And takes away
Whatever is omnipresent
Sitting in me like vibrant twins
Whatever makes me itch
Sends me to epilepsy
But delicately
Whatever is too much
For me
Too much for my bones
To hold
And so I must
Move under its pressure
Or be crushed
Whoever is real
Whoever has blood

Of earth and heaven
Whoever has eyes...
Eyes like horizons
And infinite
Whoever cares with tears
Sincere like hunger
Whoever feels
Me
As I am to be felt
Whoever sees
Transparent what is solidly
Synthetic
And values
What is simply genuine
Whoever feels love
And does not run
Love runs through
Many cities
And dresses like a bum
Whatever is human
I love
Look at me
Take my hand
One is selfish
Be two

Fast Girls Wear Loud Colors

PERIOD OF REINVENTION

Stolen sister
My face in the water
What I feel in days to come
Is what I've felt before
Habits to break can never
Be broken
Habits to make can never
Be made
Dirt and spit combine
To form my lungs
My carbon base hardens
Into raw diamonds
At the base of the mountain
I loved
And a fault line shook
Metropolises apart
I loved
And the towers crept back
Up
Up
To the sky again
But I can't find her
Among all the frivolousness
On my desk
I see her face briefly
In the crowd
Beauty
And then
Silent

NOTIONS

"I love you"
Doesn't seem to matter.
It rolls off your stone face
To the floor
Like wetness in the summer
Is it that you don't care?
Or that you are unlearned
Of the ways to paint
A woman the color
Of a kiss?
I think that when you
Shed your self-concocted
Notion of a man
You will reach your
True self
And you will love yourself
And me

BURIED ABOVE GROUND

So many girls
Love to be in love
We search until we find
Someone to bury us
Above ground
And even in silt
And Carolina red mud
And clay
We still reach
One calcified hand
Towards him
For acceptance
So many days
We lie down in our
Own graves
Waiting for him
To make us Jesus
Only that third day
Doesn't come
That third day doesn't come
And we decompose
And when the lysis sets
In our cells
Then we turn around
Like Lot's girl
And wind blows us
Down the stream
To salt the ocean
So many boys
Lite on us like hummingbirds

And bees
Fertilizing things
Sipping, sipping
And flying, flying
Migrating
To Veracruz or maybe Ghana
Before the ground freezes
And there we lay
A shard of polar
In the ground
And long forgotten
So many girls are in love
With love
So many girls wait
And wait by the door
For him
And that cold draft
Slips up their skirts
Through those pink petals
Soft as naivete
Leaves a withered rose
So many girls should
Shut that door
And warm themselves
In front of the love
In their own stoves
In their own homes

LITTLE THINGS

My life is
A little thing
To you

My arms hold
The Amazon, Sahara
So many landforms
And things

But my life
Is a little thing
To you

My hair is
Parted, twisted
To one side
Like red ocean water
Falling down my back
Like the first spring shower
And I'm naked now.

And my life
Is a little thing
To you

My skin is transparent
Bronze-gold coasts
I see canals
Like Panama

So many birds
Flying through my
Veins

My life is a
Little thing
To you

Between my legs
I grow orchards
Peaches sticky with
A glowing juice
Plums erotic forbidden purple
Pears moist and
Never bitten
My hands sink
Below my Carolina clay
And rain paints me
With those stains
Ever rolling hills
Green, then those
Sororal purple pinks

So my life
Is a little
Thing
To you

I see the blue sea
I drown sweetly
I am down
Water
Water
Watered down
To the bottom
 Of the sea
See
I see
That my life
Was a little thing
To you
What a fool

DEDICATED TO JACKSON:
THIS IS WHAT I HOPE TO TEACH

I want you to learn
That you have
Nothing to be ashamed of
And everything to be proud of

Learn that love is everything
Love is power
And with knowledge and God
You can touch anything
And make it yours

Learning doesn't end
Past the waxed gym floors
Cafeteria dishes
Of beef nuggets and tacos
And teachers that seem
To cut off the circulation
Of your youth from flowing
Through your veins
But it only begins

You are an ever-growing
Evergreen
Full of surprises
And miracles
And one-of-a-kind things

Those tests you take
In those months better spent
Running through sprinklers
And eating plates of affection

Fast Girls Wear Loud Colors

Grilled nicely on a warm day
Those tests...
Can't measure your preciousness
Or tell you of your destiny

Never let anyone
Take away your Green
Get all you can of Love
Life and
Knowledge
And rise up past the sky
To be bigger than the world
 So many hands
Try to keep you
From leaving
To be larger than that
Crushed seed
That tepid minds
Need you to be

THE ONE AFTER ME

I hold this
It rests on the creases
The riverbeds of my
Hands
Something waiting
Something standing by
Listlessly
Shining and glistening
Silver and precious
Pieces pressurized
Carbon
A jewel that bleeds
As it cuts
Stand still one day
Hear it scream
The most exquisite
Music
Because I loved
I loved with what
I had
And what I had
Yet to get
And what I'll never
 Get
I loved...

Like Atlantic, Pacific,
Indian, Artic Oceans,
Circular and complete
I loved...
As a black hole
Guiding matters near me
Gravity pulled them deep
I loved...
Like hydrogen does oxygen
And I lost
More than I had
And everything I'll
Never get
I was a virgin when
I met you
And I hope that
Knocks at the doors
Of your soul
I waited for you
And I'll haunt you
For the rest of her life

RED FLAGS

You said you saw
Red flags
During our conversation
Basically
I'm a night terror
Black widow
Waiting to hatch
Maybe the flag you saw
Was the hourglass
On my back
Red Flags
Or maybe they were
Red Lights
Stop
No yellow between red
And green
Just stop
I am a daughter
I am a sister
And a teacher
But a student
I am a cousin
A friend
A writer
An eccentric lyric
A struggle

A fear
A miracle
A juicy dreamer
A thickened plot weaver
I am a Spirit
On my way home.
Did you know me?
Did you hear me weave
My own story
In the annex of your ear?
Did you let me hang
The sparking dew diamonds
Of my life in your ear?
You've never heard of me
Before
Stop
Before you miss my life
And all your blessings
In it
Red Light
Red Flag
You abort me

CROSSOVER

He was my favorite
Type of song
Haunting and sweet
Iridescent
Translucent
Like shower doors
But not transparent
Many layers
Many colors
And I love colorful things
He was a song
I played
Again
Again
Again
Deep enough
To fertilize thought
But the surface value
Of his lyrics
Did not disturb the
Club romp
Then
He started sounding
Quite mainstreamed
Not like the unearthed

Music I knew him to be
Airplay was becoming
Overwhelming
The Billboard charts say
He's a #1
But I've lost my
Rhythm with him
Rhythmless music
Is noise
I want the haunting
Hold me in the haunting

THE DAM

You know that if you
Ever take it away,
If you ever move
One step closer
One inch closer...
You know that if
The wall falls or if
The eye and hooks
Of my bra break
And levees submit
To our attraction...
You know that if
Our irises ever fall
Flush with each other
Or if the rain ever
Beats your skin as
Hard as it does
Mine during a random
Passionate...
You know that dam
Will break
And all that love
Will come running
Down my legs
Again
Like waterpaint
Color
And you'll be swept
To the delta
Like Mardi Gras
Damn

MYSTERY IS PROTECTION

A mystery
Is an unknown thing
Swimming in darkness
And sometimes
The water is a clear carved
Jewel
And the night is
Only in your eyes
A mystery
Is safety
From things known,
People living...
It is safety
From unwanted
Advances
And unrequited
Actions
Safety from good intentions
And a life encapsulated

A 4-WEEK COURTSHIP

How far have we gone?
How far have we come?
What is left to be done?
When salt tracks
Are left on the
Soft faces of
Dark women yet
 To spread their petals
Wide in womanhood?

Who caused this?
Who is this?
Man or woman?
Man and woman
Whose love is real
Like a unicorn telling
Me that cereal is
Buy 1 get 1 free
At Wally World

It's not their fault
But it is their fault
Separately
His fire breath hatred
Warm baked ego
And her beautiful denial
That she is loving
A factory to store
E-Class racist

Black with pleather seats
She is so willing
To believe in She-beasts
Like cocoa wildebitches
And colorful peacock welfare hens

She is so willing to believe
That kissing a wolf yields a prince
But what I see and hear and
Live and breathe and am
Forced to digest
Is a fairytale

He's not evil
And neither is she
But their storybook is

The issue is not that you've
"stolen" our precious prince
Or that you are the wrong swatch
The issue is purity
The issue is truth
The issue is respect
I don't believe in unicorns

PAPER

Sex is very ordinary
It is a trite
Repetitive
Set of actions
That we are compelled to
By animal forces

Sex is like paper
It only becomes something
Once words and nostalgia
Scent and sound
Give it meaning
And life
Which is magic

To be known for sex
Is foolish
Rudimentary
To be known for magic
Is brilliant

But most people
Are easily satisfied
By paper

THOUGHTS IN VERSE

You weren't thirsting for me
Daily
Like you promised that you would
You didn't sip me
And let me
Trickle down your
Topaz dusted
Cherry wood skin
You didn't let me
Intertwine
And slide my droplets
Down hair shafts
In your beard,
Iridescent jewels
Suspended on your
Face so
You'll know I was
There
You didn't
Lick the sugar
Off your lips and fingers
Clean
Readying yourself
For another
Two more
 Seven more
Twenty eight more
Tastes
Of my twisted hips
My lifted rib cage
My trembles

PROMISES ON ICE

Promises on ice
A dream
Suspended in the
Frozen intricacies
Of politics
Bureaucracy
And confusion

We were promised
Prosperity
By a generation
Born from pent up
Anxieties of a
World wide war

We were promised
Life untethered
By civil unrest
And economic demise

We were told
That the golden star
Of education
Could be ridden
To any destination
Of our choosing

Fast Girls Wear Loud Colors

We went forward
Into our chosen
Institutions
Carnivals
Designed to grow us
Make us come
Into our age

This age
Is one of
Promises on ice
Iced over until the
Excuse of the hour
Has waned over
Economy
Jobs
A new world
Where my golden star
Has dimmed

Where we sit in a car
That zooms past
Our youth
Where we are cheated

We will be cheated
Until our promises
Are thawed

NUMBER 2

I feel like I
Should be chosen
From a menu
Where all the items
Are a dollar
Grease glazed
Snowy with salt
Processed
Pushed
Prodded
Pulled
Like pork from the bone
Slathered in slaw
Made to make friends
With hush puppies
On a Dixie paper plate
Chewed
Swallowed
Molded by intestines
Defecated
Devastated
That's what it feels like to be
Number 2
Violated
She was here and you knew it

Lavender/The Present

Lavender is a transformed red. It is mixed with blue disappointments. It is softened over time, through learning, through feeling. I still don't have all the answers, but I have the tools to find them. I still have not arrived, but I am en route. I still daydream. I still imagine "What If?" I know which answers I need and which answers I don't need. And the most important thing is that there's much more to learn.

HOPE

I found hope today
Wrapped up
Shivering in a corner
Bloody but not dead
Its eyes looked
Into a chrome atmosphere
And told Father it would not die
As long as tears remained
Warm and human
Like liquid ghosts
Hope said it would not die
But the day of the mechanical tear
Would be the day that would kill hope
If tears are mechanical
Then souls are mechanical
And so ends hope

FIGS

I just want to be natural
Like figs that grow syrupy
On distant trees
Or the shifting of bones
In jazz movements
I just want to be free
Freedom like the ocean
Swelling up over me
Like a perfume scent
That you can't remember
Nor forget
I want to linger on
Forever
After I'm gone
By progress of the wind
That blows my dandelion seeds
Across landscapes
Cities
Rooms
Until every person living
Can feel me between
Their skin and flesh
When my flesh is earth
I want to touch
Just slightly
Enough to make you half-conscious
And still tranquil

RAIN

My bones hurt when it rains
Like now, the sky is silver
Blue slate colored
Filled with angel tears
And as they come down
Single-file, from all directions
I rub my legs
My arms
The dull pain creeps up
Then my hands become stiff
I hate the rain
Making me feel like this
Hurts like heartache
Maybe it's not the rain

THIN AIR

Every now and then
The air gets thin
And I can hear myself
From within
The rhythm of my heartbeat

Sister my foe
I step past the electric line
And ask you why
You despise the air I breathe

Perseverance
Like black light
I know the world is
Contradictory
But on a bridge of dreams
I walk toward the end

FEAR

What is fear?
Fear is the demon
That traps you
Within the walls
Of perceived safety
And keeps you from
Drinking the freedom
Of life
But then,
Fear is Grace
Sent to save you
From yourself
Fear is precious
Fear is bondage
And it is because of
This contradiction
That I fear the sound
Of my own feet moving
Forward
But eagerly await
The next step

BLACK

I am not a Jamaican dream
Like a sunset
Saffron and gold
I am not a carnival from Trinidad
Full of candy love
And colored soul
I am not a Sierra Leone diamond
Pure clarity
Stars within black earth
I am not a lioness from Kenya
Golden queen of beasts
The huntress, poised and sleek
I am not an Ashanti chant
Vibrating indigo ink sky
Or a Bantu drum
Keeping rhythm
Mystic, divine

I am a low but sharp call
Keeping my brothers and sisters
In line on a dark railroad
I am a slave's hymn
Drifting over hills
Negro Spiritual I am

I am plum colored
Smooth and silky
Rhythmic twitches
Word twisting

Poetry sculpting
Harlem Renaissance I am
I am fire engine red
Volcanic
Like heat inferno
Radical like the tide
Unrested, unsatiated
Revolution I am
I am blue
Cool like rivers
Dove feathers
Resting gently on the wind
The breeze off the shore
Silence in a moment
King's Dream I am
I am now
I am here

Jamaican sunsets
Paint my skin
Trinidad's candy carnivals
Color my soul
I am hard, I persevere
I am pure
Like a diamond within charcoal
Earth
I am sleek like the lioness
Poised and ready,
I am a chant
And I vibrate the universe
Shaking stars,
And the black holes hear me

I am a drum
Hypnotizing you
Dance for I am rhythm
I am mysterious
Born from a blessed
Miracle
Formed on an African shore
Tried and tested
I am Black
And I rise in the east

A DEFINITION

Romance is
Friendship
With the power of
Infinity

I AM

I am the bolt
That keeps the
Wartime
Ship together
The scab mending
Skin over a
Wound
The time binding
Big, black
Holes of
Eternity
Dispersed
Among every star
Planet being
I am an essence
I am abstract
I am definite
I am tactile
Love

FLESH

I am flesh
And fleshen I fill
With dirt and lust
And fester for you
To pop
I am just a
Collection
Of hair
Sweat
Glands
Nerves
Bones
Urine
Dung
A cyst
To be cut off
From the body
Discarded
As a woman
My life is so many times
Hidden between
The cloudy smoke
Of the fornicate
As a dreamer
The irony is
That I am not
Wanted for my ideas
The jewels in the midst
Beauty of my head
But beauty that my

Glands produce
The hard sight I see
Is the brick
One dimensional
Wall
What is a man?
To me a man is
Mysterious
Like cancer
Sometimes infectious
Benign, others

I LOVE YOU

Island, I've been floating too long
Lingering, fighting first but then wanting to conceive
Open
Closed
Open
Closed
Violent are the winds that carry the seed of the weed
Everyone
Everywhere
Everything
Yoked, but not harnessed for the Goodness
Open
Closed
Open
Closed
Utopia, how many ways are there to write about love?

ON PURPOSE

I think of the face first,
Then the body
Skin tone transparent
Pearlescent
Colored sunny saffron
Bubblegum blueberry
Strawberry port wine
Pitch chocolate
And glittering pre-diamond matter
At once
Muscles stretch over bleached
Calcium frame
Fibers ripped
Then built up again
Liquid runs
Not sweat but similes
Feet grounded deep
In my nerves
Gray matter feeds you
No chicken fried steak
Greens diced up
Butter cornbread baked gold
You were blind until
I laid you down on
White sheets
Coaxed your legs apart
With inky blue black red

Fingertips
And weaved what was
Between my thighs
And my eyes
With yours
The ink that runs down my legs
Is your placenta
Your birthing water

DIVINE TONGUES

Poets speak divine tongues
Words molded, woven, welded
Whatever way created
Lightning in sugar coated
Capsules
We take them to
 Sleep
Heal
And improve
Words
That Poets speak
Are divine tongues

A LULLABYE

How can a man
Who loves his daughters
Believe in whores?
Certainly
The father of a woman child
Sees the little girl
In those urban amazons
These women know nothing
Of power and strength
Other than hands prying
Or tongues lying
To escape the responsibility
Of loving her
Because it's easier to
Cut now and
Ask questions never
However...
A man that loves his
Daughters
Always asks the right
Questions
Always takes the time
To dig for treasure
Treasures
The little things that
Make what she is
A woman

'Cause she is.
The bedtime stories are
Not pre-coital lullabies
Designed for ease
But pre-natal lullabies
Designed to ease
A man that loves his
Daughters
Could never be anything
But a man...could he?

PIXELS

All I see on my channel
Is snow
Each pixel is an idea
An idea that can't wait
To burst
And penetrate the walls
Of my mind
To become a real thing
But they won't wait
Their turn
They are not in a single
 File line
They are pushing and
Shoving each other
Out the door
Because the sign in the
Middle of the hall
Of my mind
Says run don't walk
My goal is to be
Disciplined
Enough one day
To pull these pixels
Together
To make a picture
Even if I have to pull
With all my strength
And even if I only
Make one
I want to make
My picture one day

PANIC BUTTON

Tight chest
Can't breathe
Faint pain in stomach
Turns to
Might need to vomit
Might need to faint
No need to get up
Too sleepy
Can I have five more minutes?
I hate my job
Do I have to go in today?
Leave me alone bitch
Head is feeling like
Katrina is inside
And my brain is the levee
That just broke and let
Panic rush in and sweep
All my damn neurotransmitters
Into the delta
Can't relax
I have to check to make sure I locked the door
Didn't remember if I checked or not so
I have to check to make sure I locked the door
Is the door locked?
Did I lock it?
Brain fog
Overcast
Raining down
Hot sewer water
Over my thoughts
I usually see things rosy

Now I see things brown
Drab
Head zaps
Dry mouth
Tics
Tics
Tics
Home
Stillness
I am another person some days
Glad to be home.

GRAVY

I had your bath water in the tub
Before you walked in the door
Butter spread on Hawaiian rolls
And sweet tea balanced
Perfectly with lemonade
Raspberries picked
Sugared and
 Baked
Sleeping nicely beside
Sliced peaches
A fruited pastry
Greens steamed and dressed in
Cayenne pepper olive oil
No pork in 'em
But maybe tomorrow because
You like your religion du jour
Gravy sits thickening on the stove
Like I do
Me unzipped
Sitting on the edge of
An unmade bed
Sheets bundled and wet
But sore Raisinet bruises
Hug my thighs like jeans
Since you leave ends rough
Settle this
You're comfortable now but
Tomorrow you'll be demanding
That a horn come out of my head

And I fly from here to Venus
Like Pegasus
An anomaly
Or a rarity

BLUE GREASE

Blue grease was on his hands
Liquid fossils
Petrol
Glazed his hands
Seeped into his skin
Threw his pulse off center
Out of harmony
And this must be the reason
He's so coarse with you
He's poisoned
A victim
An abused abuser
But I don't buy it
That same grease
Dripped down my fingertips
Recently
But I had enough sense
To wash my hands

INTUITION

My assumptions save me
From your recklessness
They care about what
I need
And they know I deserve better
The truth is what it is
Even if you dismiss it
As an assumption

ON ANXIETY

Who wouldn't have an anxiety disorder
Under the conditions that we live in
Today?
Where are these steel-nerved people
With impenetrable psyches?
Let's have lunch
So that I can touch the hem
Of your garment

SIGH

The worst part about
It all is
The sighs
Deep, long, breathy
Or
Short and labored
Sighs
Desperate for changes
To a pre-packaged
Day
A collection of which
Make a shrink wrapped
Life
Exasperated sighs
Passionate sighs
A sigh is
Letting go
Sometimes giving up

SUGAR

Sugar is the greatest Trojan horse
Brown, wet,
Syrup like liquor
Seduces like it intoxicates
Distracts while the virus is
Planted within
Etta said it was
On the floor
You lick the dirt and mangled bits
Up with it
Just to save that sweet hit
Your fix from waste
Her ass must be full of suga wata
His cum must be made of buttercream
The breath that we were promised
At Town Hall
Must taste like fizzy cola
On a tropical August afternoon
In the Eastern Carolina swamp.
The sickle in the air stays there
For about twelve hours
But for you it's twenty four
Waking hours aren't for punks

LOUD COLORS

Fast girls wear loud colors
This is the favorite
Excuse
Of our aunties, mamas,
Grannies
For muting themselves
In shades of
Nondescript blue
And easy to swallow
Tan and beige.
How many shades of clear are there?
How many shades of see-through?
They don't dress in the shades of Ntozake's palette
Saffron
Vermillion
Maize
Ultraviolet
NEON

MARRIAGE

The whiteness of the silk that
Flows from a bolt of fabric
In the back room of a
Cramped boutique
Seems to be more important than
The tightness of the two valves
That vows
Will suture together
And no man should put asunder
She stands there
On a velvet pedestal
With gossamer and tulle
Silk and taffeta
Satin, pearlescent baubles
And crystalline light
Dripping from her
As she takes in the view
From a three sided mirror
Of how she will look
As she floats in flush
With custom choreography
Down the center isle
Of a sanctuary
Filled with onlookers
Hungry for a spectacle
From which they can grow
Lush morsels of gossip

That will keep them nice and fat
Through the winter
She will be queen
On that day...
He stands there
Both arms outstretched
As the tailor reaches from one middle fingertip
To the other
Measuring his broadness
To match it with
A pewter colored sharkskin,
Heliotrope cummerbund
And matching bowtie
He's almost on the other side
Sealed away from nights
Standing on the edge
Of shimmering passion
With a faceless woman
Waist deep in the stickiness
Of a liquor only she would know
The remnants trickle down
His chin
Excitement
She's an intoxicating bitch
 That will cost him a lifetime
And then turn around and
Ask for a penny more
And the tightness of this
The rush of the exploit
How it hugs the shaft tightly
Mourning the loss of this

Fast Girls Wear Loud Colors

Is more important to him
Than the whiteness of
His vow to a woman
Who stands patiently
Waiting for him to finally
Totally
Unequivocally
Choose her
And tie up the narrative
With the closing credits
Of "Happily Ever After"
He pays homage to
Himself as he stands there
Blooming napalm flowers
Into a body, an experience
He plans to bury immediately
They stand there
On the edge of a covenant
That neither fully understands
She is lulled to sleep and distracted
By rhinestoned visions of grandeur
And he suffers a dementia
That inducts him into a brotherhood
Of men who are haunted
By the myth that some
Better prize waits for them
On the former side
And no one seems to be concerned about
This child in the middle
The marriage
The Purpose

The Mission
The Safe Place
The Promised Land that
Many have in name
But not in heart or in spirit
And of which
Many prove to be unworthy

BLOWFISH

You puff the issues up
Wide
The spikes on them
Seem sharp, but yet
They are dull to the touch
You put an ominous
Glaze on those issues
Seasoned with hyperbole,
Conjecture, hearsay,
Fried up good with
Pride and privileged
Posturing
You make a monster
Of me
A deep sea terror
Like mother Angler Fish
Blowfish
You exaggerate EVERYTHING
Until it is no longer
Recognizable
By its creator
You Are Scared
And you make things
Bigger than they once
Appeared
To make sense of things
That were never nonsense
The truth is
I am here
I am real
We are the only ones here

We are the real ones
But you have called
In sick too many times
Just to prolong your
 Fantasy
You can't face me
And our reality
Blowfish
You're just as small
As you once were
One on one
Moment by moment
Blow by blow
We'll get there
Just stay real
Unpuffed

WHAT ABOUT HER?

I hear you hollarin' that
Black Girls are Magic
But what about her...
What about the ones that live outside of the Academy
Who don't know what it feels like to wear a mortar board
On their heads?
What about the ones in bonnets in Wal-Mart
Shopping for buy 1 get 1 free packs of chicken wings
And orange Crush soda
Who will get on a bus to go
Back to a part of town
You'd never set foot in?
What about the ones in fight videos on World Star Hip Hop
Whose filmed bloodied assaults you help to make viral
As you tap send on a text to a friend
That describes this near murder as
"LOL!"
What about the ones who are not in your sorority
The ones who pledged the "wrong" sorority
Or the ones who refuse to kiss your ass
Because of three tackle twill letters
That you wear on an American Apparel sweatshirt?
What about the ones who are married to the men you want
Who you think you are prettier than
Wittier than
Who you think are less deserving than
You
Of a man who chose her first?

What about the ones who aren't Beyonce,
Or Rhianna,
Or whatever stranger whose life you plagiarize
Because you refuse to write the lyrics to your own life
What about the ones who you think are too light
What about the ones who you think are too dark
What about the ones who you think are too quiet
What about the ones who you think are too loud
What about the ones who you think are too gay
What about the ones who you think are too straight
What about the ones who are too much
And not enough at the same time
What about the ones who aren't
You?
What about her?
Is she magic too?

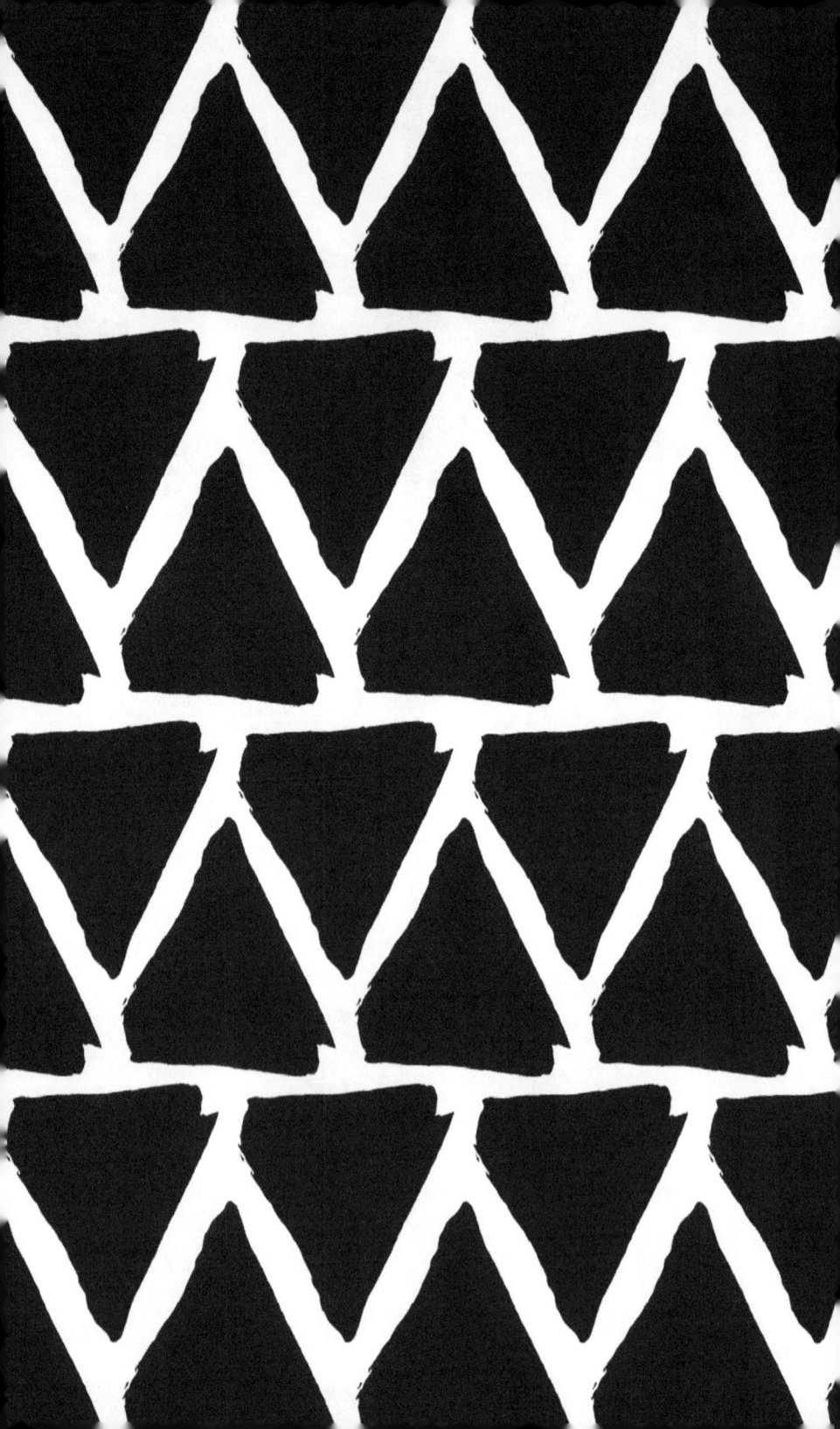

Saffron/The Future

Twilight. That's what the last years of your life are called. When
I look at an elderly woman, I see the brilliance of her life
shimmering on her skin. Moonlight. That's what bounces off
her wooly, silvered hair. That's what hides in the shadows of her
furrowed brow as she plays her life's reels in her mind. Lines. She
doesn't care for the latest antioxidant creams to get rid of them.
They are badges earned from years of laughing loudly in the faces
of those who wished her voiceless. They are stripes earned in a
world that revels in her loneliness. She calls the young girls fast.
She thinks that they are living too quickly. She wants them to
savor life and hold it in their mouths a little while longer so they
won't deprive themselves of all the colorful flavors. But the fact
is that they are living loudly like she did. They, too, will one day
have their lines where the moonlight will hide.

SURFACE GLOW

The surface glow
Is fleeting like stars
That streak across the sky
Like tear tracks
The obscurity
Leads many astray
Until they wake in their
Silveresque clouds
And find wealth
In the bloodwork
Of the soul

HANDS

When I am old
I hope to look at my hands
And see the places I went
In all the ridges of my hand
My life shall be
Fingerprint swirls
And like scrolls
They will tell of all the knowledge in my head

HOUSE OF LIGHT

House of light
Mirror rooms
Large and bright
Such an ecstasy to see
Divine and pure
Fear is a tame dog
At your door
Joy lives there
And so does Peace
With these sisters
I leave my heart
Soul and key

KISS THE SUN

I'll let you look
Into the window
To my symbolism.
Can you kiss
The sun
Without burning
Your lips?
I came in the wind
As a seed
And I landed
In the hands
 Of the earth
Seedling, sapling
One day I'll be
A big oak
Reaching up to
Kiss the sun
Burning light
No one knows
The depths of me
No one knows or sees
How the whole world
Affects one person
Or how one person
Affects the whole world
Hush now
Listen to the sky
Listen to the earth
Listen to the fire
That's the same

Color as my blood
Blood clots
Blood stops
When dead folk
Sit around drinking
Gin and whatever
Thinking
That the world doesn't affect them
And they don't affect the world
And God doesn't see them
Behind the invisible wall

LIGHTMOTHS

A moth loves light
Like we love our
Conventions
Good intentions
Intent is not movement
People under twilight
We are
Sitting among the purple darkness
Purple like bruises
Dark, bloody
Direction unknown
And unsought
This cave is frigid
Cold
Like lifeless things
But the moth
His convention
Is one that should be
Duplicated
His body dusty
Ogre like sepia color
Like dirt deep
In the gut of the earth
He's humble
Subtle
And yet with
Amber piercing eyes
Lit like candles on the alter
He flies toward the light

Fast Girls Wear Loud Colors

Is in love with the light
Forth come we from our night
Transforming blackness of the sky
To the light
Fly toward the light

SIT STILL

Sit still
Among your own shadows
Listen to the silence
The loudest song
A whole
Full note full
See
This is the hardest thing
For us to do
Sit still within the silence
Because in those moments
Long and almost measurable
By miles
We must start to think
It's the only entertainment
Available
And in thinking we begin
To think about ourselves
What we do
How we do
Where we do
Who we do
With or to
See,
We start to confront ourselves
We come to epiphanies
Not realized among
The junky noise
We
Distract ourselves with
Daily

And in confronting ourselves
We risk being
WRONG
Some people can't handle it
Some big, grown men
With rock hard bodies
And harder attitudes
Become quiet, quaint
And little
In isolation and silence
Is it the voices in our heads
Telling us the truth
Making us break our
 Crystal walls
And tarnish our golden idols?
Or is it just
Too much
Because God's voice
Comes through the silence?
So you wanna be grown
You think you're a
Force to be reckoned with?
Deal with the silence,
Deal with isolation.
Purifies like holy water
Or
Take the easy path
Turn on the TV

VINTAGE WINE

Darkness like the pit
Of passion fruit,
Arresting gem in the middle
Of the earth,
Makes the whole world
Fall mute,
Then pick up again with soul music,
Haunting, glittering sounds
Like the last hour of daylight
Colored like the first hour of twilight
So are the scat sounds
From the saxophone man,
And the deep thumps
From the bass
Her child came out that color too,
Just a darker shade
The child's sister a lighter one
Yeah, that's the shade
The shade that seeps
Down from God's hand
Through the openings between his fingers
That colors us all
Our whole history is a
Book that is covered in
Dark velvet
That the royal men wear
Majesty and humble
Are we
For this wine that touches

Our lips is our true shade
See, we are not the color
Of charcoal or chocolate
Aged and precious
Truly wine are we

Connect with Nichole O. Nichols
Twitter & Instagram: @nicholeonichols
Facebook: facebook.com/nicholeonichols
Website: nicholeonichols.com

www.ingramcontent.com/pod-product-compliance
Lightning Source LLC
Chambersburg PA
CBHW020938090426
42736CB00010B/1182